Orna Tamir Schestowitz

MEDITERRANEAN HOMES
The Art of Embracing Light

Photography by
Dudi Hasson

Text by
Beth Dunlop

New York · Paris · London · Milan

CONTENTS

THE ESSENCE OF LOCALITY
by Prof. Yael Atzmony
p. 15

PROLOGUE
p. 25

DISCOVERING JOY: A CHRONICLE OF THREE HOMES
by Beth Dunlop
p. 30

TEL AVIV
p. 37

MY HERITAGE, MY ROOTS
by Orna Tamir Schestowitz
p. 114

CAP FERRAT
p. 133

PAROS
p. 197

EPILOGUE
by Orna Tamir Schestowitz
p. 251

CAPTIONS
p. 252

THANKS AND ACKNOWLEDGMENTS
p. 255

THE ESSENCE OF LOCALITY

Orna Tamir Schestowitz's ceramics collection showcases her deep love for the land and its landscapes, expressed through materials that reflect her connection to place and creativity. These pieces are more than objects—they capture the essence of the earth, serving as both culinary and sanctuary vessels filled with the bounty of the fields.

In her "Seeds of Heritage" collection, Tamir Schestowitz brings life to vessels that embody the land's richness. Each piece reflects the spirit of harvest, moving from natural landscapes to intimate interiors. Local plants, herbs, and fruits are displayed in their natural beauty, creating authentic compositions that highlight the artist's dedication.

Her creative process is a labor of love. Some vessels stand on three legs, reminiscent of mythical creatures bearing history and culture. These designs invite touch and interaction, with textured surfaces and glazes that mirror the Earth's palette.

Tamir Schestowitz's work is further enhanced by her understanding of space and architecture. Natural light and shadows play upon the vessels, creating a seamless integration with their surroundings. Influenced by her mentor, Moshe Shek, she infuses her work with ancient forms and traditions, making each piece a timeless artifact.

Artists like Jean Cocteau, Fernand Léger, and Pablo Picasso have explored ceramics and the art of drawing on clay. Tamir Schestowitz honors this heritage with bold brushstrokes, delicate sketches, and intricate patterns that tell stories of tradition and innovation.

Years of collecting local testimonies have helped Tamir Schestowitz develop a unique design language. Her interiors and table settings blend passion with simplicity, vitality with earthiness. Each project celebrates the essence of place, highlighting the importance of locality in Israeli ceramic art.

Prof. Yael Atzmony
Chair, Department of Ceramics and Glass Design,
Bezalel Academy of Arts

"The Mediterranean is the smallest of seas, yet the greatest of wonders."

Paul Valéry

Enveloped by twenty-one European, Asian, and African countries, with 28,500 miles of coastline, the Mediterranean sea is mild-tempered—neither exceptionally turbulent nor boisterous. Seven months of the year the climate is warm, with water temperatures reaching 86°F in summer. It's pleasant here, and the winter is mild too.

The Mediterranean is not just a place, for me, it is a way of life. *It invites you to open a window and look and listen to the change of seasons, the movement of the sun that knows how to beat fiercely and set softly, to the music of cicadas, the silent murmur of the wind, the play of shadows, and the changing lights and shades. Life on the Mediterranean is harmonious, holistic, and organic. It activates all the senses—the taste of a sweet tomato ripened in the sun, the smell of the salty sea, the sweet and spicy aromas of natural Mediterranean groves with olive trees, vines, capers, and figs.*

For me, this is Tel Aviv, Cap Ferrat, and Paros—three houses, one sea: a relaxed rhythm, local colors, and special attention to the course of the sun. Yet a house in Paros cannot be like a house in the south of France or the coast of Israel. Each draws from different sources of inspiration and traditions, yet they have common traits. All three share a similar climate and characteristic vegetation. All three blur the lines between outside and inside and display affinities between light and shadow, local art, inspirations, and site-specific collections. A silent murmur of the wind. The pace is slower, attentive to nature's heartbeat.

Home is a spiritual space, the place where you feel you belong. *On the one hand, home sets boundaries; on the other, it provides an intimate and heart-opening space. Home is a place where you can simply feel comfortable. It gives you a sense of security and intimacy, it's a shelter from the hardships of everyday life. We close the door, and we are in a personal and familiar space.*

What makes that relaxed and intimate feeling?

I believe there is no single method. *The personal touch will always make a difference— the pattern of personality, the placement of furniture and art, the choice of colors, the connection to nature. Our emotional experiences are rooted there. This is the diagram of my soul.*

Opposite: VIEW FROM THE STUDIO WINDOW ON THE OLD CITY OF VILLEFRANCHE-SUR-MER

But what is the secret, the magic, that produces that often elusive feeling of calm and pleasure?

There are hidden threads that interact and create harmony. *For example, I place a sculpture that my son made in kindergarten alongside a work by a well-known artist, and between them I place candlesticks inherited from my grandmother. The invisible strands that connect the objects are hidden from view, but they are there. Those concealed threads associate a large red circle motif on an* **Alexander Calder** *tapestry with the vivid color captures in a work by artist* **Raffi Lavie***, and the same red is suddenly revealed in the upholstery of a 1950s armchair by the Italian-Brazilian modernist* **Lina Bo Bardi***. Then, too, it can also be a shape that accompanies the eye implicitly. In my living room in Tel Aviv, there is a low table designed by the Italian company Promemoria that is made of four linked amorphous bronze surfaces. It sits below randomly placed ceiling lights, and nearby are a D-Sofa by* **Ron Arad** *that continues the amorphous motif and a ceramic side table by* **Salvatore Meli***.*

This dialogue finds its expression in the spaces between the objects, between the works of art, or even in the motif—the formal affinity of the circle shape. In retrospect, I discovered many circles in my childhood drawings, and this created a deep connection rooted in the past. You don't have to decipher it, but this repetitiveness creates a pleasing harmony. After all, there is no more complete and infinite shape than a circle: it unites, just like in a circle of support. The dialogue between objects is not obvious. There are subtle affinities that are slowly revealed (or not) and eventually add peace and harmony. In music, harmony is built on the sounds of different pitches that appear at different intervals. This is exactly how my approach to design works: an encounter between elements from different worlds that together create a kind of perfection. The elements contrast—high and low, traditional and modern, colorful and monochromatic, glossy and matte. It is the Chinese theory of Yin and Yang, the two opposites that form a whole.

Connections are created in the imagination. While I am working on the design of a house, my mind wanders between the spaces, or between the drawings and plans. This is how my perception of space takes shape, eventually resulting in certainties—this chair will be placed here, and that painting must move there. I move the objects fearlessly until they find their perfect place.

When people ask what is important in design, I always say, joie de vivre, *a French term that translates as "joy of living." It embodies a joyful enjoyment of life, an exuberant and enthusiastic approach to living. This phrase is often used to express a positive and optimistic outlook, celebrating the pleasures and beauty of existence. People who embody "joie de vivre" are often characterized by their zest for life, their ability to find joy in small things, and their overall enthusiasm for living fully. It goes beyond mere happiness and suggests a deep appreciation for the experiences and pleasures life has to offer. The concept is not limited to French culture but has been embraced and adopted by various cultures around the world. It's a sentiment that encourages individuals to savor the richness of life and appreciate the present moment.*

Orna Tamir Schestowitz

THE KINDERGARTEN CERAMIC STATUE BY **FERNAND LÉGER** ASSISTED BY CERAMISTS **ROLAND** AND **CLAUDE BRICE**, 1954, FERNAND LÉGER MUSEUM, BIOT

Following spread: A MIXTURE OF ANTIQUE ITALIAN AND FRENCH CERAMICS

Discovering Joy: A Chronicle of Three Homes

by Beth Dunlop

Concepts can be elusive. Transforming the intangible into the tangible is sometimes a near-impossible task, like chasing moonbeams. Yet that is exactly what Orna Tamir Schestowitz set out to do in three houses in three different countries (and with three different cultures). The houses are in a village just outside of Tel Aviv, the small peninsula of Cap Ferrat in the French Riviera, and the tiny ancient Cycladic Greek island of Paros. Each house embraces modernity, patrimony, and history in its own way. Tamir Schestowitz is an inveterate collector. However, her intention is not to show off a museum-worthy collection of art and objects, but rather to aggregate works that are meaningful to her and that, taken together, manage to tell a story.

Born into a family that valued both authenticity and intellect, Tamir Schestowitz has followed a career path that took her from editing magazines to sculpting ceramics, along the way honing not just her eye for art and design but her philosophy and sensibility toward the potential of design and art to change lives, transform attitudes, and create community.

Tamir Schestowitz finds beauty in both the ordinary and the extraordinary and has a singular way of combining the two so that they speak to each other as if they were telling us a story. A story not just of people and places, but of the way art and design can transcend distant eras and cultures to create a single—if complex—overall vision.

Storytelling is the essence of history and culture—sometimes it is verbal, other times it is visual, such as in the case of these houses. These stories pertain, of course, to Tamir Schestowitz's life and her particular vision, which is connected both to place and time.

Certainly, it stands to reason that the story she wishes to tell starts (as many stories do) with her childhood. She was the niece of one of Israel's founders and grew up in a German-bred family that had deep intellectual interests and espoused strong values, ranging from a deep love of literature to a profound respect for the land, most particularly in terms of farming and nature, to an acute interest in archeology, in learning not just history but what we might call "history."

All of this is manifest in the three houses that Tamir Schestowitz has created—first in Tel Aviv, then in Cap Ferrat, and more recently in Paros. Each of these houses is deeply personal and yet at the same time strongly connected to its own place. The houses share a connection to the Mediterranean Sea, but they also share an overlapping ancient history with visual and written evidence of habitation over the ages, not to mention classical and modern mythmaking.

The early history of each of the three places (Tel Aviv, Cap Ferrat, and Paros) is, of course, not identical, but—like almost every spot, down to the smallest spit of land in the Mediterranean—they were claimed by the often-long-lost seafaring nations of antiquity, and the imprint remains. Thus, diverse and complex cultures reveal themselves as you dig through the layers that have evolved over the years.

For Tamir Schestowitz and her family, the primary base is Israel, a new country in a very old place. Architectural historians—especially those focusing on Modernism—think first of Tel Aviv as the White City, a reference to the extraordinary collection of Bauhaus buildings, the architecture that dominates the imagination. We think of it as a modern city—Tel Aviv was built in 1909 as a suburb of the port city of Jaffa (though now the converse is true)—but the region's history is old and long, stretching back to the Canaanites, followed by the pattern of sea conquest that dominated the Mediterranean for so many long centuries. And even today, it is shaped by forces that are both biblical and political, mythological and factual.

For these three houses in these three countries and these three cultures, the link between myth and reality is both powerful and pertinent, providing a connection of person to place and place to history and offering an artistic *leitmotif* that embraces myth and fact, fantasy and reality, past and present.

Take Paros, for example. Scientists now know that the Cycladic Islands were formed by the shifting of underwater tectonic plates thirty-five million years ago, and that the islands were inhabited as early as 3200 BC. But is that the creation story that drives the culture? Most likely not: Greek mythology tells us that Poseidon, god of the sea, became enraged by his nymphs and blew a swirling storm that caused them to turn into stone and then become islands. And the islands are so named because they form a semicircle around Delos, legendarily the birthplace of both Artemis and Apollo—a myth that remains powerful to this day.

Myth still prevails at the other end of history—modern history, not ancient—in the transformation of the south of France from what was considered a crude and even unwanted corner of the country into a sun-infused Mecca that was mysterious, glamorous, enigmatic, artistic, bohemian, and much more. The mystique attributed to the Côte d'Azur has been both minimized and elevated over the years. As Paul McCartney wrote, "The French Riviera is a place of incredible beauty and freedom. It's like living in a vibrant painting, where every day offers a new adventure in opulence and light." A more flattering descriptor—and one that Orna Tamir Schestowitz invokes in speaking of the houses in the Mediterranean—is "joie de vivre."

This phrase in itself has an intriguing linguistic and historic place in the Côte d'Azur, one that relates specifically to art history—but, as time has passed, to cultural history as well. In her seminal book, *The Invention of the French Riviera*, the American historian Mary Blume points out that the first artist to invoke the idea was Henri Matisse (1869–1954) in his legendary painting *Le Bonheur de Vivre* (1905–06), which was then translated to mean "the joy of life."

Four decades later, just as World War II drew to a close, Pablo Picasso (1881–1973) painted his much-discussed version—is it a parody? a commentary on the times?—after accepting an offer of a studio space, the second floor of the Château Grimaldi in Antibes. Picasso's painting was officially entitled "La joie de vivre ou Antipolis," a reference to the ancient Greek name for Antibes. Blume said, "The joy in the painting was real but to express it Picasso looked to the Mediterranean past. There wasn't that much joy about in 1946."

But joy there had been and joy there was to come. Soon after Picasso's perhaps sardonic painting, the Côte d'Azur was well back on its way to its own reinvention as a summer haven for writers and artists (and soon, too, celebrities and bon vivants, patrons, collectors, and more).

In 1946, Picasso happened into the atelier Madoura in Vallauris, a discovery that led to a prolific and distinctive body of work (671 pieces) over the course of twenty-seven years until his death in 1973.

Myth leads to invention and invention leads to discovery, be it by scholars or artists, scientists or explorers: the disciplines often intertwine. And this—despite the detour—brings us back to Orna Tamir Schestowitz. It is perhaps a long road from three houses in three towns in three quite different countries, but it is a road worth taking, to see how—through an artistic eye—the story not just of a family or a house or even this moment in time can be told. The essence of a particular civilization can be revealed through the objects it produces, whether they are artistic or commonplace, whether they come from the hands of a master (be it Pablo Picasso or Alexander Calder or Ron Arad—all of whom are represented in Tamir Schestowitz's collections) or from an anonymous potter or a seamstress of centuries ago making utilitarian vessels or clothing, but doing so with the love of craft and the care of creation. These, too, are in the Tamir Schestowitz collection, an acknowledgment that artistry and talent have a value—whether from the renowned or the anonymous. The connections made with style and aplomb in the three houses make art, in its broadest sense, something indispensable, the underpinning of a life full of joy.

MEDITERRANEAN HOMES
The Art of Embracing Light

TEL AVIV

"The Mediterranean light

      gives to a building a soul

that makes it alive."

Le Corbusier

Israel is a country of unexpected juxtapositions, a young, complex, and diverse land with ancient archeological and historic sites and contemporary ambitions. Tel Aviv—just next to the ancient but bustling Israel seaport of Jaffa—is one of the world's newest cities, established in 1909 to become a modern metropolis on the south shore of the Mediterranean Sea. Even the name, Tel Aviv, speaks to the dichotomies of this hilly twentieth-century city: it was taken from the Hebrew translation of the word Altneuland (the title of a turn-of-the-twentieth-century German novel by Theodor Herzl), meaning "the old new land." It was in that old new city that, in 1930, the Scottish town planner Sir Patrick Geddes embarked on an ambitious design to build not a garden city (which he was known for), but a sophisticated urban "White City" with modern, International Style buildings gleaming under the Mediterranean sun as the Bauhaus's southernmost outpost. He drew on architects who came from throughout Europe and with them, in the course of two decades, created a masterpiece of Modernism, with the largest concentration of International Style buildings anywhere,

today a World Heritage Site—a place where Modernism meets and honors the forward-thinking spirit of Israel without disavowing the country's roots or its antiquity. It was within this context that some three decades ago Orna Tamir Schestowitz built a home for her family in a village just outside Tel Aviv. From the outside, it embraces its surroundings—indeed, she calls it a "polite" house that was designed to blend in with its surroundings. It's a two-building structure with a studio for artwork and a large, open house that is intended to be a gathering place for family and friends. Step past the modest facade and you find yourself in a world of wonders, a world that embraces the cultural and artistic diversity that is Israel. This house is intended to foster comfort and conversation, while at the same time engaging the eye and the mind. It is filled with art, craft, and design, and is far from sterile. The house is intended to accommodate the immediate family and more, and to entice friends and neighbors to come, look, listen, learn, converse—and eat, enjoying the bounty of the land. If the house's exterior speaks to the traditional, vernacular architecture of the neighborhood, inside it is modern, with an open floor plan. Its furnishings are purposely wide-ranging. Fine art sits next to a child's sculpture or an archeological find. A contemporary chair by the Israeli architect Ron Arad joins other, older pieces—it blends in rather than dominates. At the center of all this is a large, long dining table, seating up to fourteen people. It is, says Tamir Schestowitz, "a place for discussion." And indeed, Israel may be a purpose-driven country, the only Jewish state in the world, but its population is drawn from many countries and cultures, from the Middle East and Eastern Europe, from the Old World and the New World. Thus, there is always room for discussion.

Opposite: BAUHAUS IN TEL AVIV: ESTHER CINEMA, 1938
Following spread: ELLA LITTWITZ'S SQUILL SCULPTURE (top left); THE HOUSE IN TEL AVIV (left); ORNA'S GRANDPARENTS' HOUSE IN BERLIN, 1929 (right)

YECHIEL SHEMI'S *PIECE OF ALTALENA*. Opposite: SCULPTURE BY **TAL SCHESTOWITZ** AT AGE NINE

Previous spread: OLIVE OIL **JARS DE BIOT** OUTSIDE THE STUDIO, NEXT TO "SEEDS OF HERITAGE" TABLES AND VESSELS

A REFLECTION OF AFTERNOON LIGHT IN THE LIVING ROOM AND KITCHEN. Opposite: A BAKHTIAR RUG, 1920, AND HANGING ART PIECES BY **SIGALIT LANDAU** AND **RAFFI LAVIE**; in the foreground: **RON ARAD**'S *D-SOFA* MADE OF POLISHED STAINLESS STEEL AND BRONZE, 1994

Previous spread: **YAIR GARBUZ**, *IF NOT A GIANT, AT LEAST IN HIS GARDEN*, 1974; BRONZE *ANIMAL* VESSEL BY **ORNA TAMIR SCHESTOWITZ** OVER AN ANTIQUE DAMASCUS CHEST WITH MOTHER-OF-PEARL EMBELLISHMENTS (LATE NINETEENTH CENTURY) AND OTTOMAN CANDLESTICKS NEXT TO A **SERGIO MOSCHENI** *GIROSCOPIO* FLOOR LAMP, 1974

CERAMIC TABLE BY **SALVATORE MELI** (1953). ON TOP OF THE TABLE, INSPIRATIONS FROM THE WORLD OF ARCHEOLOGY AND THE DEAD SEA. THE WOOD SCULPTURE *THE MESSENGERS*, 2023, BY ISRAELI ARTISTS **MERAV AND HALIL**. ANCIENT OIL LAMPS, THE BOOK *MASADA* BY **YIGAEL YADIN**, AND A HANDWRITTEN WORK TITLED *THE DEAD SEA*, CREATED BY ORNA'S FATHER IN 1934. ON THE FLOOR, A BRONZE STATUE BY **ORNA**. ABOVE, *RED FLOWER* BY **RAFFI LAVIE**

Opposite: **LINA BO BARDI**, *TRIDENTE* RECLINING ARMCHAIRS, 1950s

Following spread: *COMMITTEE TABLE FOR 14 PERSONS*, DESIGNED BY **LE CORBUSIER & PIERRE JEANNERET** FOR THE CHANDIGARH ASSEMBLY, 1963–64; *OFFICE CANE* ARMCHAIRS, MADE IN 1955 BY **PIERRE JEANNERET** FOR CHANDIGARH; **ALEXANDER CALDER**, HANDWOVEN *STAR* TAPESTRY, 1975; CEILING LIGHT FIXTURE BY **STUDIO BBPR**, 1962

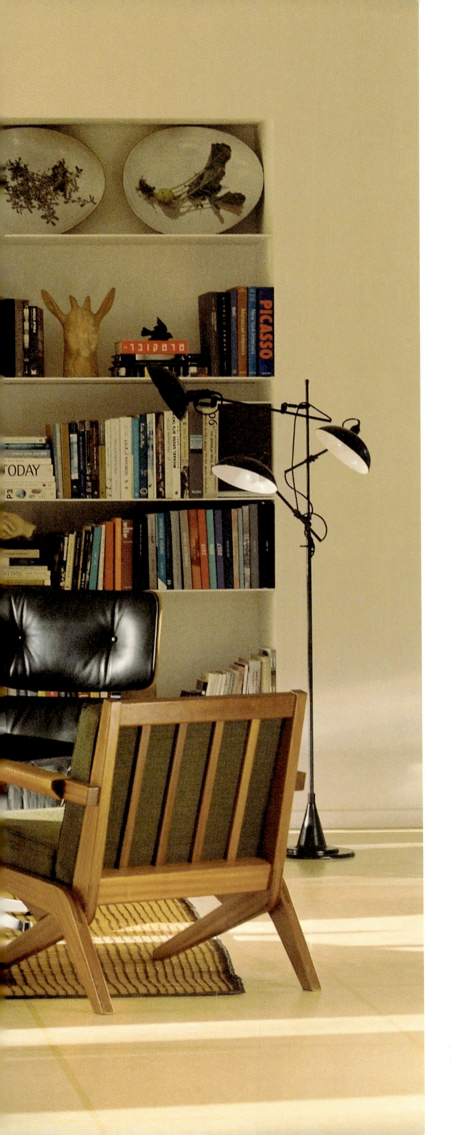

READING NOOK NEXT TO THE FIREPLACE. *BOOMERANG* ARMCHAIRS DESIGNED IN 1950 BY **OLAVI HÄNNINEN**; TWO LEATHER **EAMES** CHAIRS; ON THE MANTELPIECE, A CERAMIC STATUE MADE BY ORNA'S SON **TAL** AT AGE SIX AND A CERAMIC VASE BY **YEHEZKEL STREICHMAN** FROM THE 1950s

AN 1854 HEBREW BIBLE THAT HAS BEEN IN THE FAMILY FOR GENERATIONS. TWO PLATES THAT ECHO SHAVUOT HOLIDAY TRADITIONS: CERAMIC PLATE BY **CHEF MARC VEYRAT** (left), **MOSHE SHEK & RAFFI**'S PLATE (right). A PAINTING MADE BY **ORNA** AT AGE SEVEN

ORNA IN THE STUDIO, WITH SHELVES DISPLAYING HER CERAMIC CREATIONS

"SEEDS OF HERITAGE" VESSELS COLLECTION

Previous spread: **TAMAR GETTER**'S *AND THE CAPTAIN SAID*, 1992, HANGS ACROSS A BRONZE STATUE BY **ORNA** ON THE KITCHEN ISLAND; ON THE LEFT, A PLETHORA OF PLATES COLLECTED OVER FORTY YEARS LINE ON THE BAY WINDOW, INCLUDING SOME INHERITED FROM **ORNA**'S GRANDMOTHER, PLATES FROM TURKEY, IRAN, JAPAN, AND ARMENIA, JUGS FROM FRANCE, AND PORCELAIN DINNERWARE COLLECTION MADE BY **ORNA**

"THE ARTIST AND THE MODEL": IN THE FOYER, **JOSEPH ZARITSKY**'S *ACCORDING TO PICASSO*, 1982, AND **OLAVI HÄNNINEN**'S *BOOMERANG CHAIR*, 1950; ON THE ENTRANCE WALL (left), A WORK FROM BOGOTÁ MADE UP OF SIX CERAMIC TILES SHARES THE SAME MOTIF

Previous spread: BETWEEN THE ENTRYWAY AND THE KITCHEN, IN THE CENTER, *GROWTH* BY **MICHAL NE'EMAN**, 1980; PIECE BY **MOSHE KUPFERMAN**, 2000. ANTIQUE TAILOR'S TABLE AND A 1880 BAKHTIARI RUG

VIEW FROM THE STUDIO TO THE ENTRY LEVEL: **MERAV AND HALIL**'S SCULPTURE *THE ARCHAEOLOGIST*; ON THE LEFT, THE PAINTING *HOME LV3* BY **LARRY ABRAMSON** FROM 2017 AND ONE BY **YECHIEL SHEMI** FROM 1989

AMORPHIC BRONZE TABLE *MOSCOW* BY **PROMEMORIA** UNDER HANDMADE BRONZE SPOTLIGHTS

Opposite: STUDY DESK AND CHAIR BY **HANS J. WEGNER** (*DESK WITH TWO DRAWERS*, 1970); AN ANATOLIAN KARAPINAR RUG FROM THE EARLY TWENTIETH CENTURY, MADE OF FELT AND WOOL, HANGS ON THE WALL NEXT TO TWO PAINTINGS BY **YAIR GARBUZ**; SPREAD OVER A BERBERIAN STRAW MAT, AN **ALEXANDER CALDER** TAPESTRY FROM 1975

POPSICLE MAN, MADE BY **ORNA** AT AGE EIGHT

Opposite: IN THE BEDROOM, *DIVER 1* BY **DEGANIT BEREST**; *GENUINE PAIR* BY **GINO SARFATTI**, AN **ARTELUCE** WALL-MOUNTED PENDANT LAMP (MODEL 194/N), C. 1950, HANGING OVER AN OLD YACHT STYLE END-TABLE

INHERITED GERMAN PLATES FROM THE 1920s (left); UZBEK BUKHARIAN PLATES, 1920 (right);
A PLATE BY THE ISRAELI SCULPTOR **MOSHE SHEK** (top right)

Previous spread: PORCELAIN "SEEDS OF HERITAGE" COLLECTION, 2021, ALONGSIDE OLD FRENCH JARS

Following spread: AREMENIAN PLATE, 1920s; TURKISH POT, PRE-ATATÜRK ERA; ITALIAN CARAFE ALONGSIDE MIXTURE OF DIFFERENT PLATES

"My design approach blends diverse elements—high and low, traditional and modern, vibrant and subdued—creating a unique harmony, much like the Yin and Yang principle."

"A blend of Iraqi, Druze, and Yemenite pita breads—an ingathering of cultural flavors in Israel."

Following spread: VIEW OF THE TEL AVIV BEACH PROMENADE

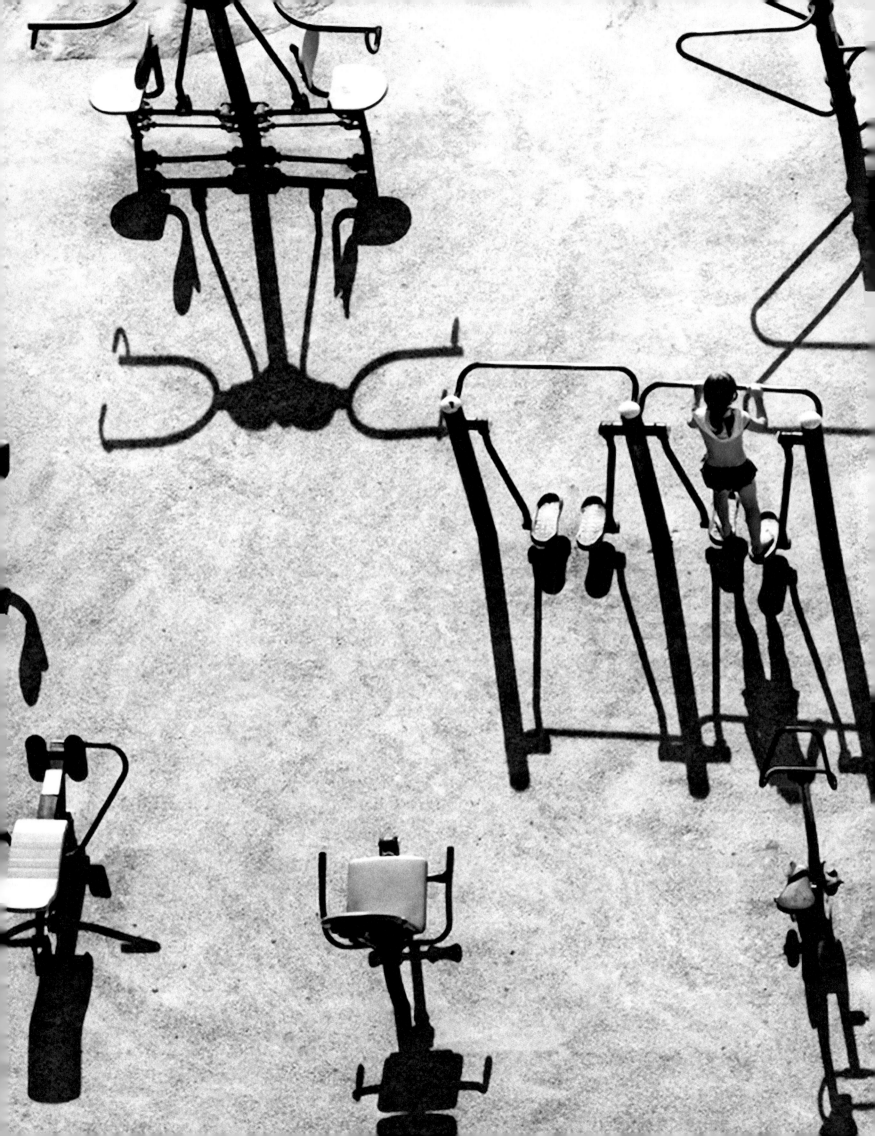

THE "SEEDS OF HERITAGE" PROJECT HAS EXPANDED ITS REACH TO THE LOWEST POINT ON EARTH—THE DEAD SEA

Previous spread: THE ILANA GOOR MUSEUM IN OLD JAFFA, OVERLOOKING THE MEDITERRANEAN SEA, WAS INSPIRED BY ITS FOUNDER, WHO WAS RENOWNED FOR HER INFLUENCE IN FOSTERING LOCAL CULTURE AND HERITAGE

"SEEDS OF HERITAGE" PLATES AFLOAT IN THE DEAD SEA

"AS I BEGAN TO RESEARCH THE SEEDS OF ISRAELI HERITAGE, I REALIZED TO WHAT EXTENT THE MAGNIFICENT PROFESSION OF AGRICULTURE WAS BEING UNDERMINED."

My Heritage, My Roots
by Orna Tamir Schestowitz

Throughout history, humanity has always worshipped the sun. In Hinduism, it is revered as the divine force present in everyday life, while Canaanite culture depicted the sun as a Goddess. Egyptian mythology, however, viewed the sun God as a symbol of evil, as it traversed the fiery depths of the underworld. Similarly, the Inca and Aztec civilizations worshipped the sun as a deity, recognizing its vital role as the prime source of life.

THE DANCE OF LIGHT AND SHADOW

When sunlight is obscured, shadows emerge and shape our perception of the world. Nowhere is this more evident than in the Mediterranean region, renowned for its luminous and intense light—a unique quality that profoundly influences the colors, shapes, and textures of the landscape. Indeed, light defines the very essence and form of objects. The interplay of light and shadow serves as the fundamental principle, the guiding force of architectural design.

> "The interplay of light and shadow serves as the fundamental principle, the guiding force of architectural design."

Blessed with abundant sunshine for over eight months of the year, the Mediterranean area faces the challenges of scorching temperatures, often exceeding 100°F. In response, a culture of shading has evolved in the form of pergolas, vine arbors, patios, and verandas. These architectural elements blur the boundaries between indoor and outdoor spaces, offering refuge from the harsh glare of the sun.

Light has always been integral to Mediterranean architecture, exemplified by the Mashrabiya—a lattice structure crafted from wood or concrete. Serving as a barrier between the exterior and interior, the Mashrabiya filters sunlight, casting ever-shifting shadows that dance with the sun's movement. Over time, these ancient features have evolved, with modern interpretations like those of the French architect Jean Nouvel at the Institut du Monde Arabe in Paris, where Mashrabiya feature apertures that adjust to the intensity of light.

A well-designed architectural plan harnesses natural light, optimizing its use based on the sun's trajectory. As sunlight filters through, it creates a mesmerizing interplay of light and shadow, casting a spell of enchantment over the built environment. This dynamic relationship not only serves practical purposes but also imbues spaces with a captivating aesthetic allure.

CERAMICS: BEAUTY MADE TO SERVE

Ceramics have been a fundamental axis in my life. My parents took me to archeological excavations where I discovered the magic in pottery, in ancient tools that revealed thousands of years of history. My children went to ceramics classes, and their works from kindergarten and elementary school are dispersed around the house, as an integral part of the art collection. For me, ceramics embody a connection to a place.

Yearning to touch the material, I came to the studio of Moshe Shek, a sculptor and ceramic artist who researched the ancient pottery traditions. He was a man of the land and believed in the symbiosis between people and the land they live on. These were inspiring teachings. We toured the country, becoming acquainted with ancient ethnic techniques.

I started creating large vessels, sometimes with amorphous shapes. The clay made from soil and local sand resulted in authentic roughness. From the very outset, I was drawn to large formats, ones that could contain ideas and images. The vessels I create are always large, concave, with a womb-like presence, and often with three legs—a receptacle that invites and embraces ideas.

Ceramics is first and foremost a useful and functional art; its decorative role is secondary. I have collected from around the world large jugs that were used to store olive oil or wine, ouzo bottles used by sailors, special molds for cheese. The bowl has a particular significance in the food culture of the Levant. In Israel, as in many Levant countries, it is customary to serve food in central vessels to make eating a joyful shared experience. Bowls with fresh, locally produced salads, local cheeses, and bread are placed in the middle for everyone to reach out and fill their plate. This is the way I usually host. It liberates, creates spontaneity, and reinforces the sense of belonging.

"My parents took me to archeological excavations where I discovered the magic in pottery, in ancient tools that revealed thousands of years of history."

PORTRAIT OF UZI TAMIR, ORNA'S FATHER

SEEDS OF HERITAGE

Heritage seeds are primary seeds, passed down through generations of farmers, that have not undergone genetic modification or hybridization. By promoting the use of heritage seeds, we can build a more resilient, sustainable, equitable food system. These seeds have important cultural, environmental, and economic significance: they preserve genetic diversity (I've learned that there are more than four thousand varieties of rice!) and are necessary for collecting, organizing, and transmitting culinary history and traditions. As I began to research the seeds of Israeli heritage, I realized to what extent the magnificent profession of agriculture was being undermined.

I went back to the studio. I created a three-legged vessel made of local clay and sand, resulting in a grainy and rough texture. After visiting a number of agricultural farms and the Volcani Institute, which is the largest institution in Israel engaged in agricultural research, I understood what was going to fill my vessels: all the goodness of the land, vegetables and fruits and herbs that have not undergone engineering or cloning, crops that were local to the Mediterranean—figs and olives, vines and grapes, cactus bushes, dates, and pomegranates. Together with a photographer, I set up a studio in the field. We photographed kohlrabi that had just been pulled out of the ground, fresh green onions, radishes, lemons at their peak, ripe pomegranates. It was a long process that considered the seasons and the short period of time when each vegetable and fruit is at its best. These images were then integrated into the vessels.

The "Seeds of Heritage" project was presented as an installation of seventy vessels at the Fresh Paint Fair in Tel Aviv. They sold out on the first evening. I tried to understand what it was about "Seeds of Heritage" that triggered sentiment in the audience. To some, it was reminiscent of childhood, a family trip, a backyard garden. These contrasts and connections aroused emotion, a longing for the days of innocence, for something that had been there once but was now gone, a taste of the past. It was a longing for the organic, for the authentic, for the local.

A SERIES OF "SEEDS OF HERITAGE" PORCELAIN PLATES

"The 'Seeds of Heritage' project was presented as an installation of seventy vessels at the Fresh Paint Fair in Tel Aviv. The installation elicited emotional responses of reminiscence and nostalgia from the attendees."

Memories and readings, the domesticity of everyday life and travels, family and togetherness: conversing with Orna is akin to delving into a sea of imagery, where her inspiring guiding principles always resurface. Let's discover them.

1. LIVING BY A GARDEN

Beth Dunlop: *You are fervent about agriculture, seeds, and gardening. Can you describe the powerful role the garden plays in your life?*

Orna Tamir Schestowitz: "Terroir" is an idea I live by. I always eat local—as fresh and organic as possible. I always see what the farmers' market offers and plan that day's meal and table accordingly. I love to decorate my tables with fruit or vegetables. I choose one particular type of produce and that serves as the jumping off point for the whole table setting, with a color palette that matches the season, the sun, and the view. In Paros, I always eat local fish such as sardines, sea bass (*lavraki*), and other catch of the day; Greek dishes (such as *tzatziki*, *dolmades*, or *spanakopita*), a lot of figs, homemade jams from the garden. And everything is always accompanied by a glass of *souma* (the local ouzo of Paros).

2. CONNECTIONS ARE EVERYTHING

BD: *You have a unique eye for the way the art and objects you own are placed. Can you elaborate on that?*

OTS: The way I place objects is individual, intuitive. I have no interest in one style, in obvious harmonious compositions. I like to break conventions and, for example, place a statue made by my son Tal when he was six next to a vase by Yehezkel Streichman. Only in retrospect do the delicate lines link—a recurring pattern of circles, seen in Tal's clay work, through

Streichman's creations, and extending to Raffi Lavie's painting above the mantel. The compositions are self-evident, and only a posteriori do the connecting threads reveal themselves.

3. HOME IS NOT JUST A FOUR-LETTER WORD

BD: <u>You have strong feelings about the differences between a "house" and a "home." Can you discuss your philosophy about the importance of home?</u>

OTS: Home is not just a physical space. To me, it's a spiritual space. It's where you belong, where you have roots. It's a place of security and intimacy, where you can express yourself freely and be what you truly are. As architect Renzo Piano stated, the house is the most important building in the world. It is not enough that it is beautiful; you have to feel good in it, experience a sense of contentment. A home is a place where people feel safe, comfortable, and connected to their surroundings.
It's a reflection of the inner world of its residents.
The best-designed houses are those that are influenced by place, climate, and the social context in which they take root. They must maintain a scale that is informed by relations with those around them, while at the same time creating their own identity and presence.
In every home, the private and public dimensions must be intertwined, without one overpowering the other.
It is precisely in our modern, chaotic world, as people seek to find a sense of stability and belonging, that the home has taken on more meaning.

BD: *<u>Although you're a fan of Le Corbusier's work and teachings, your feelings about a house differ from his idea of "a machine for living," correct?</u>*

OTS: Le Corbusier focused on the functionality of the house, whereas for me, a house is an emotional and spiritual concept. Beyond being a residential structure, a home is the place where we feel protected—it's "the heart," and this is true anywhere in the world, whether it is a nomadic tent or a spectacular villa. I took the idea of functionality and a living unit and assimilated emotions into it. A home is the place where we accumulate experiences, memories, family events, ceremonies, hosts; among its rooms we feel pain and we feel joy. This is the most intimate place. I believe that a home can shape our identity through experiences and memories.

4. THE HEALING POWER OF DESIGN

BD: *<u>Can you talk about the importance of design, not just in place-making but in shaping our lives?</u>*

OTS: Design influences our well-being. There is something comforting and peaceful about beauty, affecting who we are and making us happier and more attentive. When the design is right it is also comfortable, inviting, embracing: a veritable balm for the soul. For instance, when I design a library with a cozy reading nook, I am also encouraging the family to read. The house abounds with meaning when we pour the personal into it—that is, the objects in the house are indifferent, it is consciousness that gives them value. My home is in Israel. I was born here, built my family here. My roots are here. Each item in the house symbolizes a piece of memory, an experience from a trip, from a private moment. A Biedermeier accent heirloom table passed down through my husband family, a painting by my daughter, plates I inherited from my grandmother, a dresser from my parents' house. The more layers there are, the deeper the meaning. This emotional space cannot be copied, it is completely personal, private, protected.

5. UNDER A SHELTERING SUN

BD: <u>*Can you define the meaning of life near the Mediterranean?*</u>

    OTS: As I shared, the Mediterranean is not just a place, it is a way of life. It is a relaxed and attentive lifestyle that takes into account the seasons, the light, the sun, the local vegetation. It is a harmonious, holistic, and an organic mode of existence, one that is wholly connected to the place. The Mediterranean lifestyle is a celebration of the senses—the taste of good food, the smell of the sea, the warmth of the sun, and the beauty of nature. The boundary between outside and inside is permeable. The outside enters the house through large windows; the inside flows outside through balconies, patios, and pergolas.

6. EMBRACING LIGHT

BD: *The Mediterranean is known for its very particular sunlight, which has lured artists and poets and writers to its shores for not just centuries but millennia. What enchants you about the light there?*

OTS: I myself have a complex relationship with the sun, as I have sensitive skin. I'm always looking for shade. But in designing, light brings joy, reveals the truth. Light is a crucial element in the Mediterranean—the least expensive and most important raw material. Light is a critical component of architecture. It's not just a question of illumination, it's a question of how light communicates with structure, how it defines the spaces and shapes. The light of the Mediterranean Sea is not only brightness: it's the interplay between light and shadow that creates the depth and complexity of the architecture in the region. I love natural light; that is why I choose large windows that let it in, eliminating any barrier between the inside and the outside. Light creates an atmosphere, sometimes a mystery, which is generated and defined by shadows. It inspires calm and peace, depth and drama.

7. THE ART OF PROPORTION

BD: *Are there particular aspects of architecture and design that intrigue you?*

OTS: Small or large, far or near, dense or spaced, wide or narrow: there is no single answer. Finding the right proportions is the secret of good architectural design. Proportion is balance, and balance is the essence of beauty, not a matter of personal taste.

It is an objective principle that governs any good design, a language that requires skills and a precise eye. Proportion is the key to achieving harmony and beauty in architecture, if we want the final result to be more than the sum of its parts.

8. PLAYING WITH SHAPES

BD: *What themes are recurrent in your design?*

OTS: In my childhood paintings that my mother has kept, it is evident that the circle is my favorite form. The circle is a perfect shape, mirroring a whole life cycle—just like the sun, the moon, the earth. It is a natural form, one harmonious and complete unity. Without beginning and end, the circle symbolizes universal, unlimited, eternal energy. Later, the perfect shape of the circle came to represent an inclusive unit, a support circle. The spirals are open circles, without end, allowing release toward infinity. These appear throughout my residences in various forms—lamps, art, tapestries. The perfection of the circle is contrasted by free-form, or amorphous, shapes. These are shapes devoid of order, with greater inner freedom. From the bronze table in the living space in the Tel Aviv house to Ron Arad's abstract version of a sofa to brush paintings on hand-made plates—amorphous shapes are a recurring element in my style.

"THE VESSELS I CREATE ARE ALWAYS LARGE, CONCAVE, WITH A WOMB-LIKE PRESENCE, AND OFTEN WITH THREE LEGS—A RECEPTACLE THAT INVITES AND EMBRACES IDEAS."

BERBER MOROCCAN BUTTER-CHURNING VESSELS

Opposite: A BRONZE VASE DESIGNED BY **ORNA TAMIR SCHESTOWITZ**

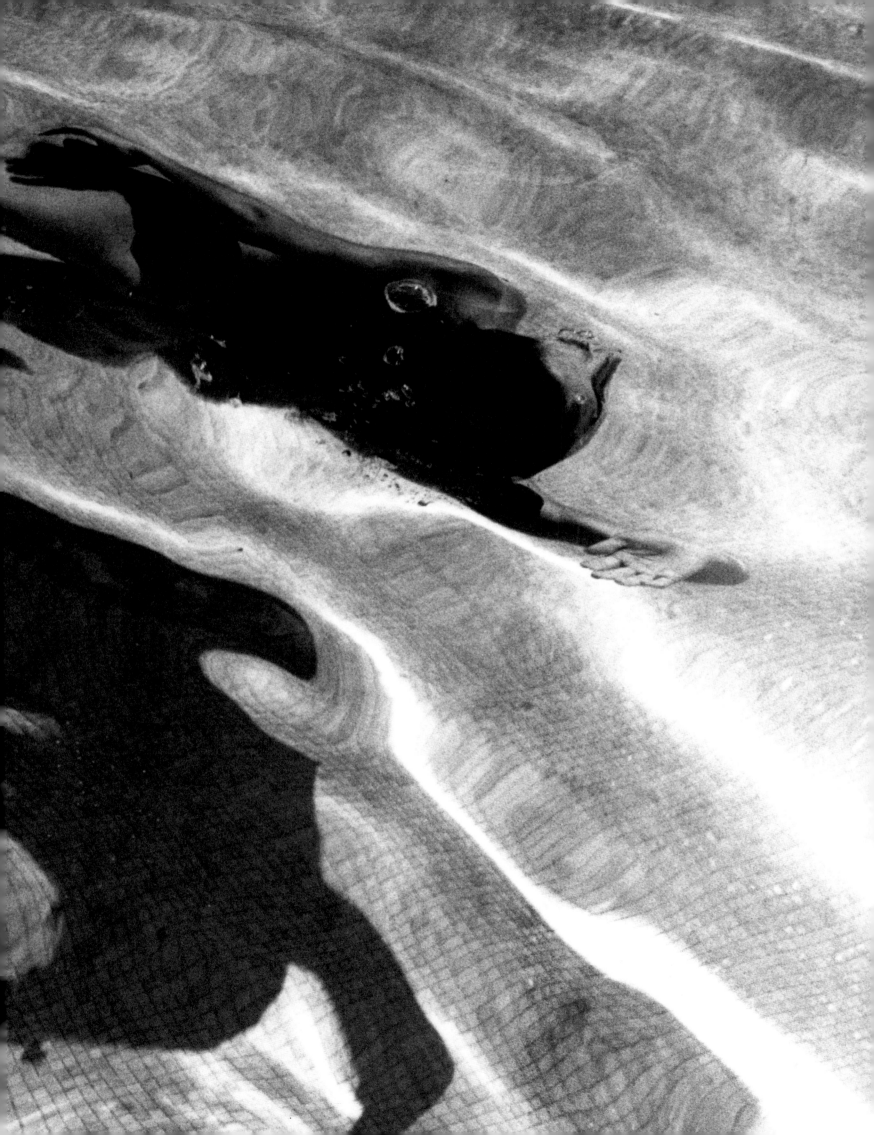

CAP FERRAT

"I have always loved the Mediterranean.

It is the sun of a country that has given me colors, light, a way of living."

Henri Matisse

On the map, this part of France undulates along the Mediterranean coast, curving like a sideways S, and even from that bird's-eye view, the possibilities abound and tease the imagination. Most commonly, this southeasternmost part of the country is called the French Riviera; more poetically, it is the Côte d'Azur—a reference to the juxtaposition of sea and sky, an apt appellation because, translated, the word azur (azure in English) means, very specifically, "sky blue." Neither name truly conveys the dramatic beauty of this specific and special part of France, which has for generations—really even for centuries—entranced and attracted visitors (from ancient Greeks and Romans on the move through Europe) to the poets and writers, artists (Picasso, Chagall, etc.) and architects, and those who have been drawn there for more than two centuries now (up to eight million tourists a year). **Still the list of creative and intellectual people drawn to the South of France—to Nice, Antibes, Saint-Tropez, Cannes, Vallauris, Cagnes-sur-Mer, Vence, Menton, Villefranche-sur-Mer, Cap Ferrat, and more—seems almost endless**, like a college curriculum in nineteenth- and twentieth-century art and literature: the names would fill volumes.

Some came and went, others just visited, but still others laid down roots and, in their writing and painting, sculpture and architecture, helped define the Côte d'Azur of the late twentieth and early twenty-first centuries, capturing and perpetuating in words and images, and even in buildings, the remarkable allure of this spectacularly beautiful sun-drenched corner of the world. It was more than twenty-five years ago, on one of her many trips—one might even call them pilgrimages—to the South of France that Orna Tamir Schestowitz happened upon a house built in the 1960s that reflected the sensibilities of some of the powerful architectural forces that had shaped the modern Riviera—Le Corbusier, Eileen Gray, Charlotte Perriand, Josep Lluís Sert, and even Oscar Niemeyer. The house she found overlooked the bay of Villefranche-sur-Mer, connecting land, sea, and sky. It was long and thin, with a V-shaped roof that looked like a bird in flight. She redesigned it along with the Israeli architect Orly Shrem in the spirit of French Modernism: the result was a transparent house with thin bronze-framed windows, which she filled with color—the blues of the sea and sky, the greens of the lush vegetation, and reds and oranges to reinforce the vibrant spirit that pervades the environment—adding character to a house where antique furniture from local flea markets and antique shops sit side-by-side with the modern. Much like the Tel Aviv house, it is filled with art, including her large, longtime collection of Modernist ceramics (including works by Pablo Picasso, Jean Cocteau, Roger Capron) as well as antiques and objects from Tamir Schestowitz's wide travels. It is strongly connected to the spirit of the French Riviera, but it is also a crucible of ideas, a place for conversations and cultural exchanges. A house meant to foster connections to the land and to art, where family and friends can enjoy and appreciate it all.

Opposite: **LE CORBUSIER**'S *CABANON* OVERLOOKING THE MEDITERRANEAN SEA IN ROQUEBRUNE-CAP-MARTIN

"The Mediterranean is my air, my light, and my landscape. All I need is this to create my work."

Eileen Gray

EILEEN GRAY AND JEAN BADOVICI'S *VILLA MODERN E-1027*, 1924, IN ROQUEBRUNE-CAP-MARTIN

Previous spread: CAP FERRAT TOP-FLOOR BEDROOM OVERLOOKING THE BAY THROUGH SLENDER-FRAME, HANDMADE BRONZE WINDOWS; TWO **EAMES** *ALUMINUM GROUP* LOUNGE CHAIRS; **EILEEN GRAY**'S *TROIS* TABLE AND *MÉDITERRANÉE* RUG FROM THE LATE 1920s

A RED-TOPPED MEMPHIS LAMP BY **ETTORE SOTTSASS**, 1982, NEXT TO A TAPESTRY BY **ALEXANDER CALDER**; BURMESE WOODEN DRUM COLUMNS; 1970s RED ARMCHAIRS

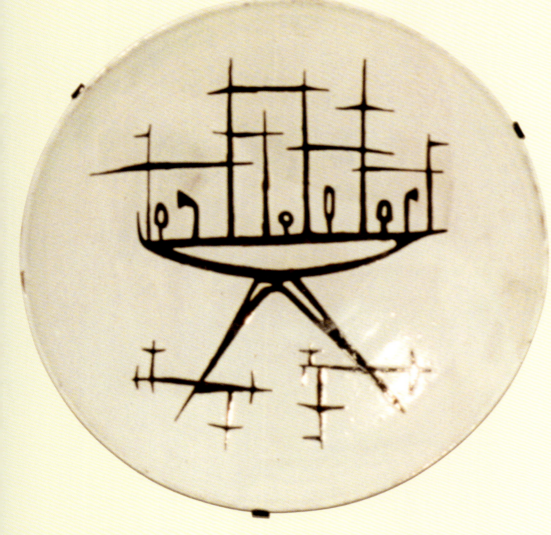

ALEXANDER CALDER'S *LOMBRIZI* TAPESTRY, 1975

Opposite: REFLECTION THROUGH THE MIRROR LAMP OF TWO ARMCHAIRS FROM THE 1970s, CANDLESTICKS BY **ARIK LEVI** AND, IN THE BACK, A WOODEN LADDER FROM MALI

HEADBOARD IN THE BEDROOM WITH A DISPLAY OF VASES BY ARTISTS INCLUDING **RON ARAD** AND **JEAN COCTEAU**, A FISH BY **PICASSO**, A VASE FROM VALLAURIS, COMBINED WITH LAMPS FROM THE 1960s

Opposite: **GRETA MAGNUSSON-GROSSMAN**'S *GRASSHOPPER* FLOOR LAMP, 1947

Previous spread: STUDIO OVERLOOKING THE BAY: **EILEEN GRAY**'S *COLLAGE* RUG; **GAE AULENTI**'S *PIPISTRELLO* LAMP, 1965, ON A MID-CENTURY SCANDINAVIAN WRITING DESK

"I like objects made by man—say, a factory stove or the tableware one uses to set a table. The stove is the fruit of a collective effort, like a painting. The potteries of Madoura are the fruit of a collective effort. I want to live among them as one lives among paintings, in a universe of space and light."

Pablo Picasso

LE SEIN DE NOUNOU CHEESE WITH FRESH FIGS ON PLATES FROM VALLAURIS

Top: SELECTION OF LOCAL CERAMICS. Bottom: REFLECTION OF CŒUR-DE-BŒUF
TOMATOES IN A STAINLESS STEEL BOWL

OFFERING RECONCILIATION

In the early years of this century, terrorism became routine in Israel. The Intifada claimed thousands of victims on both sides: soldiers and civilians, Jews and Palestinians. The area was bloody. One of the victims was Captain David Damelin, a graduate student in philosophy: in 2002, a terrorist opened fire killing ten soldiers, including David. His mother, Robi Damelin, a peacemaker and owner of a public relations office, joined the Parents Circle—Families Forum, an organization of more than five hundred bereaved Israeli and Palestinian families, and began the struggle for reconciliation, an effort to show that pain belongs to the attackers as well as to the attacked. Robi Damelin sent a letter to the terrorist who shot her son saying that she saw him, too, as a victim of the struggle. I was touched by this power, and when she asked me for assistance on behalf of the Forum, the idea of "Offering Reconciliation" was born. I created a model of a large, symbolic, womb-like vessel that could contain a variety of ideas, and cast 136 of them. The identical unadorned vessels were handed over to prominent Israeli and Palestinian artists—including painters, sculptors, designers, and photographers—with full freedom to express their own interpretation of the meaning of reconciliation. "Offering Reconciliation" was initially displayed at the Ramat Gan Museum of Israeli Art. Former World Bank president Sir James Wolfensohn visited the exhibition and donated one quarter of a million dollars to share this message of peace with wider audiences. The exhibition, also underwritten by AIDA (Association of Israel's Decorative Arts), was first shown at Brandeis University before traveling to the World Bank in Washington, D.C., the Bellevue Museum in Washington state, the United Nations, the Pomegranate Gallery in New York, and finally the Sculpture Objects Functional Art and Design Fair (SOFA) in Chicago. A year later, all the vessels were sold at Sotheby's and the proceeds were donated to the Family Forum's educational activities.

Opposite: PLATES BY **GIDI RUBIN** AND **DAVID REEB**

PAROS

"Mediterranean light—that means light, gaiety, health, brightness, all that one is entitled to expect from the sun."

Jean Cocteau

Over the centuries (actually over the millennia) Greece has inspired the great creators—writers, poets, playwrights, philosophers, sculptors, painters, architects. Greece gave us mythology, and to this day, its cities and villages and landscapes are the stuff myths are made of. And still today, the siren call of Greece and its legendary islands is beckoning. In his book *My Family and Other Animals*, the writer Gerald Durrell spoke of "the bright, looking-glass world of Greece," and indeed, from the brilliant blue hue of the sea to the sun glinting off the sparkling marble-clad and white stucco buildings, there is magic at work. This was his first memory, his first sight of Greece: "The sea lifted smooth blue muscles of wave as it stirred in the dawn-light, and the foam of our wake spread gently behind us like a white peacock's tail, glinting with bubbles." Greece is truly a country of the sea, with—depending on how one counts them—as many as six thousand islands and islets, of which fewer than two hundred are inhabited. **Among the latter is Paros, an island less celebrated than some of its neighbors (such as Mykonos and Santorini), but nonetheless an ancient and important place, with evidence of settlement dating back to 3200 BC.**

It is a small island (just thirteen miles long and ten wide), and yet over the centuries it has been under Cretan, Dorian, Aegean, Persian, Macedonian, Roman, Venetian, Turkish, and Greek rule. Thus, it is filled with historic architecture that reflects this rich and diverse history. The marble found on Paros was used to make the Venus de Milo and Nike of Samothrace, two of the most famous sculptures in the history of civilization. In a way, this small Cycladic island still speaks today to that civilization. Both understated and famous, it is celebrated for its food, its archeological and classical history, and for that very special, everlasting Greek allure. It is known for its sites and dramatic sights, both natural and man-made—ancient, medieval, and modern. It is also known for its bountiful gastronomic offerings, and for its fierce wind blowing from the sea. In conjunction with the local architectural firm G&A Evripiotis, Orna Tamir Schestowitz built a modern house that faces the crystal-clear Aegean waters. It is a low, wide house surrounded by a stone wall that encircles it protectively from the frequent sea winds. The architecture, though of its own time and consciously using local materials, reflects the island's history and its architectural vocabulary without copying it, and much more. The house also embraces the climate, the culture, and the local agriculture, bowing to the island's abundant and diverse agronomy. It has inner courtyards, patios, pergolas, and abundant gardens with lemon, apricot, plum, fig, pomegranate, carob, and olive trees, grape vines; and, closer to the ground, capers, eggplants, herbs, and spices. Obeying the local regulations and in recognition of the power of the wind, the windows are small—nonetheless, the views of the sea are omnipresent. It is a house strongly connected to place, filled with antique Greek clothing, remnants of the seafaring life (like a bright yellow fish net), artifacts of history such as Jewish dowry boxes from Athens and Thessaloniki, and more. The living room is dominated by a straw and rope tapestry by Alexander Calder—the indoor colors intentionally not the expected blues and whites of Greece.

Opposite: SLIDING WOODEN DOORS OFFER PROTECTION FROM THE STRONG CYCLADIC WINDS
Following spread: AN INSPIRING COMPOSITION FEATURING **VANGELIS KYRIS** AND **ANATOLI GEORGIEV**'S EXHIBITION CATALOGUE *RAIMENT OF THE SOUL*

UNDER THE STRAW PERGOLA, WHICH FILTERS SUNLIGHT INTO PATTERNS OF LIGHT AND SHADE, THE GRAY LOCAL STONE IS HIGHLIGHTED. THE FRONT RELAXATION PATIO, WITH ITS TRANQUIL COLOR PALETTE, ENHANCES THE NATURAL BEAUTY OF THE CYCLADIC STYLE. ON THE WALL, VESSELS FROM THE "SEEDS OF HERITAGE" COLLECTION

THE CENTRAL PATIO: TWO LONG TERRAZZO TABLES AND CACTI PLANTED IN ANCIENT GREEK OLIVE OIL JUGS

"I adhere to principles of authenticity and locality by placing bowls of fresh, locally sourced dishes in the center for everyone to enjoy. This approach celebrates terroir and local produce, creating a warm, spontaneous dining experience that fosters a strong sense of belonging."

Previous spread: TOMATOES FROM THE ORGANIC GARDEN, LOCAL CHEESE FROM THE ADJACENT ISLAND OF NAXOS, PORCELAIN PLATES FROM THE "SEEDS OF HERITAGE" COLLECTION

GREEK ENTRYWAY. THE OLIVE TREE, A TIMELESS EMBLEM OF PEACE SINCE ANCIENT TIMES, CARRIES DEEP CULTURAL AND SYMBOLIC IMPORTANCE IN MEDITERRANEAN HERITAGE

THE DESIGN OF THE HOUSE DRAWS INSPIRATION FROM THE HARBOR, AS THE YELLOW FISHING NET INTERACTS WITH THE WARM GOLDEN HUES INDOORS.

PETROS BRINGS THE HEIRLOOM HERBS HE GATHERED FROM THE GARDEN

PAINTING MADE IN TEL AVIV BY **ORNA** AT AGE TEN

Opposite: BRINGING IN FIG BRANCHES, BOUGAINVILLEA, AND FRESHLY PLUCKED GARDEN FLOWERS TO BRIGHTEN UP THE INDOORS

A GLIMPSE INTO THE LIVING AND DINING AREAS WITH MONOCHROMATIC SCHEME: BUILT-IN BOOKCASE ALCOVES DISPLAYING **AKROKERAMO**, 1880–1920; GREEK NEOCLASSICAL ELEMENTS FEATURING MYTHOLOGICAL MOTIFS; ON THE TABLE, SOUMA FLASKS AND TRADITIONAL SMALL STRINGED MUSICAL INSTRUMENTS

Previous spread: THE SEAMLESS TRANSITION FROM THE LIVING ROOM TO THE PATIO: **BBPR** ARMCHAIRS DESIGNED FOR THE LIBRARY OF CASA COZZI IN 1943; ON THE WALL, **ALEXANDER CALDER**'S *TURQUOISE* TAPESTRY, 1975

ALEXANDER CALDER'S *SUN* TAPESTRY, 1975, ITS VIBRANT YELLOW AND CIRCLES ECHOING THE SHAPE AND COLOR OF THE FISHING NETS AT THE HARBOR; A COLLECTION OF ANCIENT GREEK JUGS

A CURATED COLLECTION OF FUNCTIONAL ART: VINTAGE OUZO BOTTLES
FROM THE 1970s AND CERAMIC JUGS

A VIEW FROM THE DINING AREA, ADJACENT TO THE KITCHEN,
THROUGH THE LIVING ROOM TO THE OUTDOORS

THE DINING ROOM FEATURES NARROW SEA-FACING WINDOWS, AN AMORPHOUS WOODEN TABLE, AND A UNIQUE ROPE LAMP DESIGNED BY **ALVARO CATALÁN** AND CRAFTED BY A SOCIAL PROJECT IN AFRICA; ADJACENT IS A STAINLESS-STEEL KITCHEN ISLAND TOPPED WITH FRESH GARDEN FLOWERS

THE DOWRY BOX SHOWCASES EMBROIDERED TRADITIONAL CLOTHES, SOME WITH BOLD THREADS. ON THE WALL HANGS A PIRPIRI, A NINETEENTH-CENTURY FORMAL DRESS COVER FROM IOANNINA, EPIRUS

> "The best design is the simplest that works."
>
> Richard Feynman

LOOKING OVER THE MEDITERRANEAN FROM **EILEEN GRAY** AND **JEAN BADOVICI**'S *VILLA MODERN E-1027*

In my reflective epilogue, I recount of a fascinating thirty-year journey across the Mediterranean, which has deeply touched my soul. From vibrant markets to ancient landscapes and serene fishing villages, each place has left an indelible mark, instilling in me a profound appreciation for simplicity and beauty.

My exploration of Mediterranean architecture and design has transcended mere professional endeavor; it has been a symphony of senses—a dance of colors, scents, and the ever-changing play of light and shadow that defines this enchanting region. Beyond its physical allure, the Mediterranean embodies a way of life that resonates deeply within me—a life imbued with warmth and authenticity found in every town square, in every sun-drenched corner.

For me, the Mediterranean is an idea, a philosophy shaped by the relentless sun and the timeless rhythms of nature. This realization has captivated my imagination, echoing the creative spirits of ancient Greek mythmakers and modern artistic luminaries such as Pablo Picasso and Henri Matisse, who found inspiration in its boundless hues and ethereal light.

Central to my narrative is a deep emotional connection to Mediterranean light—the gentle caress that defines spaces, paints landscapes in vivid hues of warm yellows, oranges, and radiant reds, and imbues every moment with a sense of poetic wonder. Nature, in its verdant greens and shimmering blues, flows seamlessly into the homes I have designed, creating sanctuaries of peace and serenity through open windows and tranquil patios.

My journey as both editor and designer has been a quest for authenticity—a pursuit to capture the essence of place in every stroke of design. From the sun-kissed shores of Israel to the timeless charm of Paros and the artistic allure of the south of France, the homes I have crafted are not just buildings but living embodiments of a deep-rooted connection to land and heritage. They are sanctuaries where memories intertwine with art, where personal treasures and cherished heirlooms weave a narrative that speaks to the very core of my being.

For me, these designs are not just reflections of professional commitment but true repositories of emotions—a tapestry woven with threads of nostalgia, love, and a profound sense of belonging. Each room, each piece of furniture, carries with it a story—a story of childhood visits to historic sites, of evenings spent with family and friends around a laden dining table, where laughter echoes against the backdrop of local wines and flavors.

In essence, this epilogue is a heartfelt homage to the transformative power of design and the enduring beauty of the Mediterranean—a journey that continues to resonate deeply within my soul, forever intertwined with the rich tapestry of Mediterranean life and culture.

Orna Tamir Schestowitz

CAPTIONS

Tel Aviv

A VIEW OF THE MEDITERRANEAN FROM **ILANA GOOR MUSEUM** IN OLD JAFFA. HOUSED IN AN EIGHTEENTH-CENTURY BUILDING, THE MUSEUM DISPLAYS HER ECLECTIC ART COLLECTION ALONGSIDE HER OWN CREATIONS

AN IMAGE FROM THE DEAD SEA "SEEDS OF HERITAGE" VIDEO PROJECT. THE INTERPLAY OF THE INTENSE SUN RAYS REFRACTING OFF THE WATER CREATES A UNIQUE ARRAY OF TEXTURES THAT RESEMBLE LETTERS FROM ANCIENT LANGUAGES

A CLAY MASK CREATED BY MY DAUGHTER MICHAL, ALONG WITH VINTAGE SILVERWARE AND DELICATE PORCELAIN FROM THE FAMILY COLLECTION, IS PLACED ON A LARGE SAGE TABLE FROM THE "SEEDS OF HERITAGE" PROJECT

IN A VIDEO ART PIECE, PORCELAIN PLATES FROM THE "SEEDS OF HERITAGE" PROJECT ARE DELICATELY POSITIONED ON THE SALT CRUSTS AT THE DEAD SEA

ANCIENT BREAD STAMPS, HISTORICALLY KNOWN AS "PROSPHORA SEALS," ARE SHOWN ALONGSIDE A TSOTRA, A TERRACOTTA GLAZED FLASK USED FOR SOUMA, A TRADITIONAL APERITIF COMMONLY OFFERED ON AEGEAN ISLANDS AS A WELCOMING GESTURE

BAUHAUS BUILDING IN TEL AVIV, DESIGNED BY **YEHUDA MAGIDOVICH**, 1938. THE WHITE CITY OF TEL AVIV WAS DECLARED A UNESCO WORLD HERITAGE SITE DUE TO ITS FOUR THOUSAND BUILDINGS IN THE BAUHAUS STYLE—MINIMALIST ARCHITECTURE THAT EMPHASIZES THE POWER OF SIMPLICITY

Cap Ferrat

VIEW FROM THE HOUSE OVERLOOKING VILLEFRANCHE-SUR-MER. THE TOWN, FOUNDED IN 1295, WAS ONCE UNDER ITALIAN RULE, A HERITAGE REFLECTED IN THE YELLOW-ORANGE HUES OF ITS BUILDINGS. THIS WARM COLOR SCHEME INSPIRED THE DESIGN OF THE HOUSE

REFLECTION OF TWO BIOT JARS ON A WALL DISPLAYING A COLLECTION OF CERAMICS FROM VALLAURIS. THESE TRADITIONAL JARS, PRODUCED SINCE THE SIXTEENTH CENTURY IN THE TOWN OF BIOT IN SOUTHERN FRANCE, WERE USED FOR STORING OLIVE OIL

THE 1960s HOUSE HAS A V-SHAPED ROOF THAT LOOKS LIKE A BIRD FLYING OVER THE BAY OF VILLEFRANCHE-SUR-MER

VIEW OF VILLEFRANCHE-SUR-MER

COLLECTION OF VINTAGE DISHES. AN ASSORTMENT INCLUDING GREEN CERAMICS BY **JÉRÔME MASSIER** FROM 1950, A **ROGER CAPRON** PITCHER, VERRE DE BIOT GLASSES IN DIFFERENT HUES, PERNOD AND RICARD BOTTLES, SILVER HOT-COCOA TUMBLERS, AND **R. BRICE** PLATES FROM BIOT AND VALLAURIS

Paros

TYPICAL GREEK ENTRANCE, SHELTERED FROM THE CYCLADIC WINDS BY STONE WALLS, WITH AN ANCIENT OLIVE TREE AT ITS CENTER

PAROS INSPIRATION: AN IMAGE FROM **VANGELIS KYRIS** AND **ANATOLI GEORGIEV**'S *RAIMENT OF THE SOUL*, EXHIBITION CATALOGUE, ACROPOLIS MUSEUM, ATHENS, 2023. ON THE LEFT, AN ANTIQUE TERRACOTTA GLAZED FLASK TRADITIONALLY USED FOR SOUMA. ON THE RIGHT, A BACKGAMMON BOARD

THANKS AND ACKNOWLEDGMENTS

On this exhilarating quest through architecture and design around the Mediterranean, I've been graced with the unwavering support of my loving family and cherished friends.

To Yonatan, my beloved better half, our four children, and the grandchildren who bring boundless joy into our lives—thank you for your endless patience and willingness to lend a hand, whether moving furniture or sharing in moments of wonder.

And to my father, Uzi, a treasure trove of memories and wisdom who continues to guide me.

The circle has always held special meaning in my life, symbolizing completeness and the supportive circle of friends who have enriched my journey. From Chef Erez Komarovsky, my partner in the "Seeds of Heritage" project, to photographer Dan Peretz, for capturing the beauty of the Israeli sun, and Orly Shrem, an architect and kindred spirit. Limor Gorali, Mira Shachar, Yael Gamzu, and Roni Baharaff—thank you for your enlightening conversations.

Eran Zmora, who published my first book and has been encouraging me to publish another one ever since.

Many collaborators have become cherished friends along the way. Rona Speizman, the graphic designer who knows almost every frame of my life; Sonia Marmari, a dear friend who turns my dreams into eloquent words; Liv Ben Shafrut, my indispensable assistant navigating the complexities of production; architects Angeliki Evripiotis and Yannos Kourayos, who unveiled the mysteries of the Cyclades Islands; Simone Ciarmoli, a producer and art director with impeccable taste, always propelling me forward; Amon Yariv and the Gordon Gallery, custodians of exceptional Israeli art deepening my local ties through art; the Ilana Goor Museum, the Eileen Gray Museum, and Martinous Gallery; and Petros, my guide to antiquities in Naousa— thank you for making life more beautiful.

A special place in my heart belongs to the Ceramics Department at the Bezalel Academy of Art and Design, where encounters with students continuously inspire me: you are the future.

To all my friends, thank you.

And finally, heartfelt thanks to the team at Rizzoli—Francesco Baragiola, Cecilia Curti, Laura Decaminada, and Beth Dunlop—who enabled me to open this window onto the Mediterranean.

p. 57: Achillina Giuseppina Bo Bardi, *Tridente* reclining armchair © Achillina Giuseppina Bo Bardi by SIAE 2024

pp. 57, 58–59: Le Corbusier & Pierre Jeanneret, *Committee* table and *Office Cane* armchairs © FLC by SIAE 2024

pp. 58–59: Alexander Calder, *Star* tapestry © Calder Foundation, New York, by SIAE 2024

p.76: Alexander Calder, tapestry © Calder Foundation, New York, by SIAE 2024

pp. 240, 242: Alexander Calder, *Sun* tapestry © Calder Foundation, New York, by SIAE 2024

p. 156: Ettore Sottsass, *Memphis* lamp © Erede Ettore Sottsass, ADAGP, Paris, by SIAE 2024

pp. 156, 160, 162, 164: Alexander Calder, *Lombrizi* tapestry © Calder Foundation, New York, by SIAE 2024

p. 168: Pablo Picasso, ceramic fish © Succession Picasso by SIAE 2024

p. 168: Jean Cocteau, ceramic sculpture © Jean Cocteau by SIAE 2024

pp. 237, 239: Alexander Calder, *Turquoise* tapestry © Calder Foundation, New York, by SIAE 2024

p. 249: Le Corbusier, *Nemo* lamps © FLC by SIAE 2024

All images in the book were produced with the permission of the homeowner and/or museums that had the pieces in their collection at the time of the photo shoot. Every effort has been made in good faith to trace the copyright holders and obtain permission to reproduce the artworks appearing in this book. The Publisher may be contacted by entitled parties for any iconographic sources that have not been identified.

Art Direction and Graphic Design
LAURA DECAMINADA

© 2024 Mondadori Libri S.p.A.
Distributed in English throughout the World
by Rizzoli International Publications, Inc.
49 West 27th Street
New York, NY 10001
www.rizzoliusa.com

ISBN: 978-88-918411-2-4

All rights reserved by Orna Tamir Schestowitz.
No part of this publication may be reproduced, stored
in a retrieval system, or transmitted in any form or
by any means, electronic, mechanical, photocopying, recording,
or otherwise, without prior consent of the publishers.

Printed in Italy

2025 2026 2027 2028 / 10 9 8 7 6 5 4 3 2 1

Visit us online:
Instagram.com/RizzoliBooks
Facebook.com/RizzoliNewYork
X: @Rizzoli_Books
Youtube.com/user/RizzoliNY

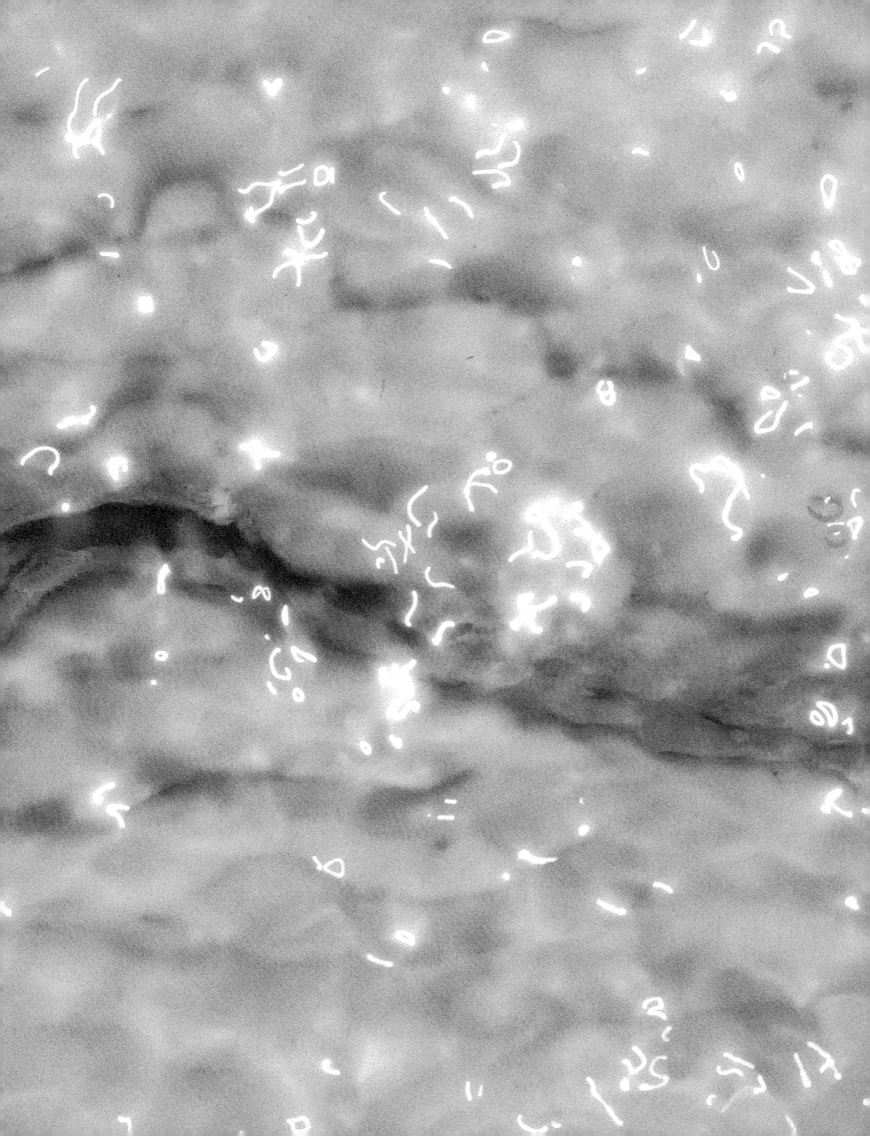